DUNDONIAN FOR BEGINNERS

The 'ch' sound on page 11 is vital.
Enjoy and practice hard!

Love, peace + laughter

Andy
xx

DUNDONIAN *for* BEGINNERS

*The Indispensable Guide
to Dundee Patter*

Mick McCluskey

WITH ILLUSTRATIONS BY

Belinda Langlands

MAINSTREAM
PUBLISHING
in association with
James Thin Bookshops

First published in Great Britain 1990 by
MAINSTREAM PUBLISHING COMPANY (EDINBURGH) LTD
7 Albany Street
Edinburgh EH1 3UG

Reprinted 1990, 1991 and 1992

ISBN 1 85158 308 4 (paper)

British Library Cataloguing in Publication Data.

This book is dedicated to all of the school-teachers who work within the
district. With the help of this book, they will now know what is written
about them on the school desks and toilet walls.

Typeset by Blackpool Typesetting Services Ltd, Blackpool
Printed in Great Britain by Scotprint Ltd, Musselburgh

ACKNOWLEDGEMENT

A special thanks to Henny King for her enthusiasm and support during the production of this book.

CONTENTS

INTRODUCTION

As with most dialects, words and phrases used by native Dundonians, change with the passing of time. *Dundonian for Beginners* has been written with one aim in mind . . . to tell it as it is. What I mean, is that the words and phrases used in this book are that of the 1990s Dundonian, and not of the 1890s Dundonian. The reader will therefore not be subjected to out-of-date phrases such as, 'Hoots mon', or 'Och aye the noo'. These ye olde sayings definitely went out with Nelson's eye, and no ordinary Dundonian under the age of 120 years, (with the exception of language graduates) would be able to tell you the true meanings of such phrases. In brief it reads as it sounds in the street today. Phonetics at its best. Before you delve deeper into this book, there are a few preparations you must do first.

TUNING YOUR EAR

This is not as simple as it sounds. Tuning your ear, unlike tuning your car, or tuning into Radio Tay, can be a long and laborious task, perhaps frightening at times. None the less, those of you with patience and determination will soon get the hang of it.

There are two stages involved in tuning your ear. These are:

STAGE I

Find yourself a bench to sit on, preferably in the City Centre, and secure all loose items of clothing. Get yourself sitting comfortably and close your eyes. By having your eyes closed, the natives will think that you are asleep and consequently leave you to your own devices, therefore extinguishing any chance of premature conversation. At this stage you will no doubt hear a variation of sounds which you already recognise; cars, buses, footsteps etc. Block out all the sounds which you recognise, (use self-hypnosis if it helps) while at the same time try to analyse the sounds which you don't recognise. As I said before, this is not as simple as it sounds. It is probably on the same par as learning to read and write. (Analysing the black bits and ignoring the white.) One of the strange sounds which you will repeatedly hear is the sound, 'Eh.' At first you might think that the 'Eh' sound is being produced by a flock of seagulls circling overhead, and you would be right, after all, they are Dundonian seagulls. To be able to distinguish the difference between the Dundonian seagull 'Eh' and the Dundonian human 'Eh' you will either have to totally wipe out all seagull colonies within a sixty mile radius, or instead, use the more simpler method . . . Move on to stage II.

STAGE II

For this you will need a pocketful of small change and a newspaper.

First, find a suitable bus and climb aboard. Late-night buses are undoubtedly the best choice. Any destination will do, although I'd strongly suggest that you take an inland route, as the river routes are usually full of migrant Dundonians who continually sing their national anthem, 'The folk in the schemes can kiss my foot, cause I'm a fo-oreman'.

Having found the right bus and climbed aboard, find an empty seat, sit down, and pretend to read your newspaper. Avoid using an out-of-date newspaper, as this might draw undue attention.

Fare paid and newspaper raised, you can now begin tuning your ear. Start as you did in stage I, only this time there won't be any seagull 'Eh' sounds to distract you. Try to lock into a conversation which is going on near you. In other words, eavesdrop. A mother and child conversation is best at first, gradually progressing in easy stages until you eavesdrop the ultimate conversation between 'Twa ald wiyfeez.' Once you have found yourself 'tuned' into the ultimate conversation, take care not to let yourself become too engrossed in what the natives are actually talking about, or you might find yourself alighting the bus prematurely just to catch the end of a story.

This is definitely not a wise move. Stay within the safe confine of the bus.

Stages I and II complete, you will have an ear which can pick out individual Dundonian words at a thousand paces.

Now to try it for yourself.

PRODUCING THE 'EH' SOUND

Place a tourniquet around the throat, just above the adam's apple and tighten briskly. As soon as you are unable to breathe, summon up a dainty little cough and clear your throat. There, you have just sounded the word 'Eh', no doubt like a true local.

Practise the 'Eh' sound as often as your larynx will allow, and then practise some more, just to be on the safe side. It shouldn't be long before you're an expert. After all, Dundonian babies are sounding 'Eh' before they stop breast feeding.

'Eh' by itself, can be translated in three ways. Firstly, 'Eh', meaning, 'Eye' as in, 'Uv sumhin in mi eh!' Or, 'Eh', meaning, 'I' as in, 'Eh hay sumhin in mi eh'. And finally, 'Eh', meaning, 'Yes' as in, 'Eh, eh hay sumhin in mi eh'. As you can see, the three meanings of 'Eh' can be used both individually and collectively.

There are many Dundonian words which incorporate the 'Eh' sound, which, with a small amount of practice, and a greater amount of bravado, even a child could learn.

Let's begin with a few single syllable words.

D. for Dundonian,   E. for English.

D. BEH .... E. BUY.

SINGULAR	PLURAL
Eh'll beh.	Wull baith beh.
Ee'll beh.	Yooz beh.
Shull beh.	Thay'll beh.

11

D. DREH .... E. DRY.

SINGULAR	PLURAL
Um dreh.	Wir dreh.
Eez dreh.	Yoo dreh.
Shiz dreh.	Thir dreh.

D. FLEH .... E. FLY, CUNNING.

SINGULAR	PLURAL
Ehm fleh.	Wir dead fleh.
Eez fleh.	Yoor fleh.
Shiz fleh.	Thir fleh.

D. FREH .... E. FRY.

SINGULAR	PLURAL
Eh'll freh.	Baith o' wi ull freh.
Ee'll freh.	Yull freh.
Shull freh.	Thull freh.

D. HEH .... E. HIGH.

SINGULAR	PLURAL
Um heh.	Wir heh.
Eez heh.	Yir affy heh.
Shiz heh.	Thir too heh.

D. KREH .... E. CALL.

SINGULAR	PLURAL
's meh kreh.	Wull baith kreh.
's heez kreh.	Shoor kreh.
's hur kreh.	's thair kreh.

12

D. LEH .... **E. A LIE.**

SINGULAR

Uv telt a leh.
Eez tellin a leh.
Shi saiz it's a leh.

PLURAL

Wuv lehd.
Yir tellin lehz.
Thir ah sayin it's a
 leh.

D. PEH .... **E. A PIE.**

SINGULAR

Eh'll hay a peh.
Eez hayin a peh.
Shiz hayin a peh.

PLURAL

Wull baith hay pehz.
Yooz kid hay a peh.
Thir ah hayin pehz.

D. TREH .... **E. TRY.**

SINGULAR

Eh'll treh.
Ee'll treh.
Shull treh.

PLURAL

Wull treh.
Yull treh.
Thull treh.

D. WEH .... **E. WAY.**

SINGULAR

Meh weh.
Hiz weh.
Hur weh.

PLURAL

Oor weh.
Yir weh.
Thir weh.

It would be helpful to suck a mint while reciting the last exercise. It helps to disguise any trace of a foreign twang which your voice may already possess.

A SPECIAL NOTE

Mint sucking during the singular and plural exercise may have some unpleasant side effects for some readers. The first symptom of singular and plural mint sucking is very easy to spot. This page should be drenched in saliva. If you feel embarrassed about all this newly-accumulated spit, you should practise in the solitary confine of your own room.

N.B. You may also benefit by keeping a large bucket and a pile of paper-hankies near at hand.

LEARN THE ALPHABET
THE EASY WAY

A is fir Aipul.
B is fir Ba.
C is fir Crabbit, jist liyk mi gran'da.

D is fir Dockay.
E is fir Ehrum.
F is fir Fleg, thit miyt day yi hehrm.

G is fir Glaikit.
H is fir Hail.
I is fir Inglish, yi git tot in skail.

J is fir Joogul.
K is fir Kent.
L is fir Lahray, whut's bumpirz ir bent.

M is fir Mingin.
N is fir Nut.
O is fir Oxtir, thit swehts kwiyt a but.

P is fir Payvee.
Q's obsolete.
R is fir Rah, liyk a fresh siyd o' beef.

S is fir Sannayz.
T is fir Threed.
U is fir Umpteen, if it's loads thit yi need.

V is fir vext.
W's fir Wah.
Y is fir Yella, like non-drinkin snah.

Z is thi last ain, an that's fir Zitno.

An that iz thi alfibit, so ull say cheerio.

15

SOME BASIC EXPRESSIONS

D. for Dundonian,   E. for English.

Dundonian	English
Eh.	Yes.
Nut.	No.
Tah.	Thank you.
Cheerz.	Thank you very much.
Sah riyt.	That's all right.
Nay bahthir.	You're welcome.

GREETINGS

Hiya.	Hello.
Moarnin.	Good morning.
Eftirnain.	Good afternoon.
Y' ahriyt.	How do you do.
No bad.	I'm very pleased to meet you.
Whut like?	How's it going?
Whut like?	How are you?
No bad it ah. Yirsel?	Very well thanks. And you?
Whut?	Excuse me. (I didn't hear.)
Whut joo say?	I beg your pardon?
Oot mi road.	Excuse me. May I get past.
Nay bahthir.	That's quite all right.

17

Dundonian	English
Cheerio.	Goodbye.
See yi eftir.	See you later.

QUESTIONS

Whar?	Where?
Wharz?	Where is?
Whar ir?	Where are?
Wha?	Who?
Whut?	What?
'ji meen?	What do you mean?
Whut?	Which?
How?	Why?
Yir awa ahed o' iz.	Could you speak more slowly?
Gohnna riyt it doon?	Please write it down.
Ji ken?	Do you understand?
Eh dinna ken.	I don't understand.
Eh ken.	I understand.

WANTING . . .

Eh wahnt.	I'd like.
Wi wahnt.	We'd like.
Ji wahnt?	What do you want?
Show iz . . .	Show me . . .
Show iz it.	Show it to me.

Dundonian	English
Geez.	Give me . . .
Geezit.	Give it to me.
Um stehrvin.	I'm hungry.
Um chokin.	I'm thirsty.
Geez.	Bring me.
Geez it owir.	Bring it to me.
Eh dinna ken whar eh am.	I'm lost.
Um buggird.	I'm tired.

THERE IS/IT IS . . .

Thirz . . .	There is . . .
Thir ir . . .	There are . . .
Zir . . .?	Is there . . .?
Zir . . . ?	Are there . . . ?
Sowir thair.	There it is.
Thir owir thair.	There they are.
Thir izna.	There isn't.
Thir irna.	There aren't.
Thirz nay . . .	There isn't any . . .
Thirz nain.	There aren't any.
It iz . . .	It is . . .
Snoh . . .	It isn't . . .
Fund it.	Here it is.
Fund thum.	Here they are.

CAN . . .

Kin eh hay . . .?	Can I have . . .?
Kid wi hay . . .?	Can we have . . .?

19

Dundonian	English
Kid yi show iz . . .?	Can you show me . . .?
Ji ken . . .?	Can you tell me . . .?
Whut wiy iz it ti . . .?	Can you direct me to . . .?
Eh canna.	I can't.

IT'S . . .

Ehrlay/Lait	Early/late
Chaip/Deer	Cheap/Expensive
Riyt/Rang	Right/Wrong
Ful/Empy	Full/Empty
Bonny/Hackit	Beautiful/Ugly
Heer/Thair	Here/There
Fest/Slow	Fast/Slow
Ald/Nyoo	Old/New
Beh'ir/Wurs	Better/Worse
Big/Wee	Big/Small

QUANTITIES

A wee drap.	A little.
A drap.	Some.
Loadz.	A lot.
A piyul.	Many.
Inuff.	Enough.
Mair.	More.
Eny.	Any.

A SPLASH OF USEFUL DUNDONIAN PHRASES

These are not arranged alphabetically, but under subject headings.

D. for Dundonian, E. for English.

PUBLIC TRANSPORT

BY TAXI

D. Wharulla git a taksay fay?
E. Excuse me, where can I get a taxi?

D. Gohnna git iz a taksay?
E. Please get me a taxi.

D. Hoy!
E. Taxi!

D. Whudz it cost ti . . .?
E. What's the fare to . . .?

D. Tak iz ti . . .
E. Take me to . . .

D. Geez a hand wee mi cais.
E. Could you help me with my luggage.

D. Drehv doon thair.
E. Turn at the next corner.

D. Jino ken it's thurtay in thi toon mait?
E. Could you drive more slowly.

D. Lit iz oot.
E. Please stop here.

BY BUS

D. Wharulla git a bus inti thi toon?
E. Where can I get a bus into town?

D. Whut bus ji git fir . . .?
E. What bus do I take for . . .?

D. Wharz thir a bus stop?
E. Excuse me, where is the nearest bus stop?

D. Much iz it ti . . .?
E. How much is the fare to . . .?

D. Yull hay ti hay thi riyt cheenj.
E. You will need the correct change.

D. Um gayin iz far iz thi toon.
E. I am going as far as the City Centre

D. Huv eh got ti cheenj?
E. Do I have to change buses?

D. Mehny stops iz it?
E. How far is the journey?

D. Yull hay ti nipit if yir biydin doonstairz.
E. Smoking is only permitted on the upper deck.

D. Zis bus gohn ti Kir'in?
E. Does this bus go to Kirkton?

D. Yull hay ti cheenj busiz in thi Heh Street.
E. You will have to change buses in the High Street.

D. Tell iz whar ti git aff.
E. Will you let me know where to get off?

D. Lit iz aff.
E. Please let me off at the next stop.

D. Abdee aff.
E. All change.

CAR RENTAL

D. Geesa . . .?
E. I'd like a . . .?

D. Wee moh'ir.
E. A small car.

D. A fehmlay sehz moh'ir.
E. A large car.

D. A fehst ain.
E. A sports car.

D. Ain thits no bahd on joos.
E. An economical runner.

D. Kid eh git it fir . . .
E. I'd like it for . . .

D. A cupla dayz.
E. Two days.

D. A lang weekehnd.
E. A bank holiday weekend.

D. A fohrtniyt.
E. Two weeks.

D. Much?
E. How much is the rental fee?

D. Zira miylij chairj?
E. Do I have to pay extra for mileage?

D. Whut aboot thi pehtrul?
E. Is petrol included?

D. Yi wahntin inshoorins tay?
E. Do you require insurance cover?

D. Fulay cohmp.
E. Fully comprehensive.

D. Lits hay a decko it yir lehsins?
E. May I see your driving licence?

OUT AND ABOUT ON FOOT

D. Wharulla git a map o' thi toon?
E. Where can I buy a good guide book?

D. Zira toorist plais aboot?
E. Is there a tourist office nearby?

D. Wharaboots?
E. Where is it?

D. Wharz/Whar ir thi . . .?
E. Where is/Where are the . . .?

D. Bitahnikull gairdinz.
E. Botanical gardens.

D. Cairdee.
E. Caird park.

D. Cahmpay.
E. Camperdown Country Park.

D. Coort.
E. Courthouse.

D. Coonsul buldin.
E. Council buildings.

D. Doontoon.
E. Downtown area.

D. Ehrt collij.
E. Artists quarter.

D. Foontinz.
E. Fountains.

D. Krehmay.
E. Crematorium.

D. Lehbray.
E. Library.

D. Monyimint.
E. Monument.

D. Stobee.
E. Stobswell area.

D. Swahnay panz.
E. Stobsmuir Park.

D. Sweengz.
E. Children's play park.

D. Tiy.
E. River Tay.

D. Toon hahl.
E. Town hall.

AT THE RESTAURANT

D. Yordirin yit?
E. Are you ready to order?

D. Ell hay thi ta'ayz, staik peh an peez.
E. I'll have the potatoes, steak pie and peas please.

D. Mi plaitsa clortay.
E. My plate is dirty.

D. Thi biyuld hamz aff.
E. The cold meat is not fresh.

D. Twa peh suppirz an a singul peh.
E. Pie and chips twice, and a single pie please.

D. 's taistay iy!
E. Would you not agree that this meal is delicious?

D. Geez sum sahs.
E. May I have the sauce please.

D. Thi braidza foostee.
E. The bread is stale.

D. Heer pawl, wharza lahvee?
E. Excuse me waiter, would you tell me the way to the W.C.?

D. Thi gehm.
E. I have enjoyed the meal.

D. Wha'r yi trehn ti kid.
E. You have miscalculated the bill.

D. Ehm no piyin ah thon!
E. I shall refrain from paying such a large sum!

SHOPPING

D. Geeza tully.
E. An evening paper please.

D. Wharulla git it fay?
E. Where will I get it from?

D. Wharzir a boochir?
E. Can you tell me where the nearest butcher shop is?

D. Wharulla git inginz fay?
E. Where will I get onions from?

D. Eny kerrayirz?
E. May I have a carrier bag please?

D. Sinekstri fehv.
E. That will be an extra five pence please.

D. Much?
E. How much is that?

D. Sezizit?
E. What size is it?

D. Ull gee yi inithirain instid.
E. I will give you a replacement.

D. Whaz in chairj?
E. Who is in charge?

D. Jooz hay eny pehz stull?
E. Do you have any pies left?

D. Wuv nain.
E. I'm afraid we are out of stock.

SPORTS

D. Mawa ti thi futbah.
E. I am off to a football game.

D. Gohn yirsel!
E. That was a good one!

D. Cripullum!
E. Tackle your opponent!

D. Eez beein sehnt aff.
E. He is being sent off.

D. Wull yiz stop yir muckin aboot an day sumhin!
E. Come on, play the game properly!

D. Yiz shood be mallayin thum beh now!
E. You should be winning by now!

D. Yizir kikin it aboot liyk a skwahd o' ald wiyfeez.
E. Your tactics are at fault.

D. Wha wun?
E. What was the final score?

D. Wi got bait.
E. Our team lost.

D. Wi got tankt.
E. Our team lost heavily.

D. We wun.
E. Our team won.

D. Nuhinzup.
E. A no-score draw.

AT THE BEACH

D. Wharzit ahriyt ti sweem?
E. Where can we bathe?

D. Wharullwi cheenj?
E. Where does one change?

D. Wharullwi pit wir claiz?
E. Do you have a coat hanger?

D. Ji hink enybudee ull stail wir stuf?
E. Are our things safe here?

D. Zi wah'ir cald?
E. What's the water like?

D. Saffay cald.
E. It's a touch on the cold side.

D. Ehm nay gaid at sweemin.
E. I can't swim very well.

D. Ehm jist gohnna leh heer an git broon.
E. I only want to sunbathe.

D. Yir liyk a timah'a.
E. How tanned you are!

D. Eh widna sweem thair if eh wiz yoo.
E. Be careful, there is a strong current.

D. Zata keech flo'in in thi wah'ir?
E. What is that strange object floating on the water?

IN THE HOME

D. Mak yirselz it haim.
E. Make yourselves at home.

D. Yir baits ir ah guttirz.
E. Your boots are muddied.

D. Mald manz on thi broo.
E. Father is unemployed.

D. Mi mithirz go' a wee joabee.
E. My mother does part-time work.

D. Zat tee no maskt yit?
E. Has the tea infused yet?

D. 's behn thi hoos.
E. It is in another room.

D. Munkul Boabz it thi windee.
E. Uncle Bob is at the window.

D. Iz yoor Netty beh'ir yit?
E. Has your daughter Annette had her baby yet?

D. Watna peece wee yir tee?
E. Do you want bread with your meal?

D. Wah behn thi hoos if yiz ir kerrayin on!
E. Go into another room if you intend playing the fool!

D. Wull yoo no tak a tellin!
E. Enough is enough!

D. Mald manz awa fir a tully.
E. Father has gone for an evening paper.

THE CINEMA

D. Son it thi show thi niyt?
E. What is showing at the cinema tonight?

D. Kiynda fulmzit?
E. What sort of film is it?

D. Whaz it beh?
E. Who is it by?

D. Whaz in it?
E. Which film-stars are playing the leading roles?

D. Whaz thi direhctir?
E. Who is the director?

D. Zir eny saits left?
E. Are there any seats available?

D. Much?
E. How much are the tickets?

D. Gohnna stik twa tickits ti thi siyd fir iz?
E. I want to reserve two tickets.

D. Doonstairz.
E. I want a seat in the stalls.

D. Much ir thi deer saits?
E. How much are the seats in the circle?

D. Wharulla pit mi jehkit?
E. Can I check my coat?

NIGHT CLUBS

D. Whuts a brah clubbee ti go ti?
E. Can you recommend a good club?

D. Wharz yir mehmbirshup caird?
E. Are you a member of this club?

D. Di yi git in wee jeenz?
E. Is evening dress necessary?

D. Iz thir a groop?
E. Is there a floor show?

And once inside . . .

D. Huv yi piyd yir subz?
E. Have you paid your club dues?

D. Twa spehshullz.
E. Two pints of your finest draught beer please.

D. Miynd an tak a tray wee yi.
E. Please remember to take a tray with you.

D. Watna gee it soks on thi flair?
E. Would you care for a dance?

D. Awa'n keech.
E. No thank you.

D. Whazat geein eezsel a showin up?
E. Who is that man who is attracting everybody's attention?

D. Ken whaz wun thi rafful?
E. You'll never guess who has won the raffle?

D. Whaz on thi nikst roond?
E. Whose turn is it to buy a round of drinks?

D. If yi dinna hud yir weesht, yir oot!
E. Be quiet, or get out!

D. Huv yiz no got haimz ti go ti?
E. Drink up and get out.

D. Eh wiz riyt oot thi shoowin.
E. I enjoyed myself.

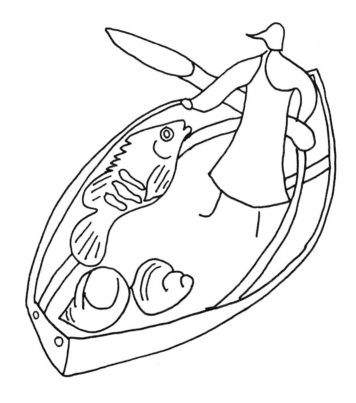

MAKING FRIENDS

INTRODUCTIONS

D. Ahriyt?
E. How do you do?

D. Yahriyt?
E. How are you?

D. No bad at ah.
E. Very well, thank you.

D. Whut like?
E. How's life?

D. Ahriyt. Whut aboot yirsel?
E. Fine. And you?

THE FOLLOW UP . . .

D. Huv yi been in lang?
E. How long have you been here?

D. Um no lang in.
E. I've been here for a short while.

D. Huv yi been heer afore?
E. Is this your first visit?

D. Nuh, um iy heer.
E. No, I come here quite a bit.

D. Sno bad in heer iy?
E. Are you enjoying yourself?

D. Wha ir yi wee?
E. Are you on your own?

D. Whar ji cum fay?
E. Where do you come from?

D. Um fay . . .
E. I'm from . . .

D. Whar ji biyd?
E. Where are you staying?

D. Huv yi go'a joab?
E. What's your occupation?

D. Cheerio.
E. See you later.

D. See yi thi moarn.
E. See you tomorrow.

D. See yi thi moarnz moarnin.
E. See you tomorrow morning.

D. See yi thi moarnz eftirnain.
E. See you tomorrow afternoon.

D. See yi thi moarnz niyt.
E. See you tomorrow night.

THE WEATHER

D. Brah day iy?
E. Isn't it a lovely day?

D. 'sbiylin iy?
E. Isn't it hot?

D. 'scald iy?
E. Isn't it cold?

D. Ji hink it ull rehn thi moarn tay?
E. Do you think it'll rain again tomorrow?

35

DATING

D. Fag?
E. Would you like a cigarette?

D. Sat yir drinkin?
E. Can I get you a drink?

D. Whut ir yi dayin thi niyt?
E. Are you free this evening?

D. Wull wi go ti thi show?
E. Shall we go to the cinema?

D. Fansy a drehv?
E. Would you like to go for a drive?

D. Eh ken a brah clubbee.
E. I know a good discotheque.

D. Fansy iz di yi?
E. Would you like to go out with me?

D. Wharulla meet yi?
E. Where shall we meet?

D. Yoor hoos.
E. I'll pick you up at home.

D. Aboot seevin.
E. Around seven o' clock.

D. Ir yi on thi fone?
E. What's your telephone number?

D. Wha ji biyd wee?
E. Do you live alone?

D. Whaz gittin yi up thi road?
E. May I take you home?

D. Doot it ull hay ti be a taksay now.
E. What time is your last bus?

D. Cheerz, it's been brah.
E. Thank you, it's been a lovely evening.

INVITATIONS

D. Watna hay yir tee it meh hoos thi moarn?
E. Can you come over to dinner tomorrow?

D. Watna cum owir ti meh hoos, uv go'a kerray-oot?
E. Can you come over for cocktails?

D. Watna cum ti mi doo?
E. I'm giving a party tomorrow. Would you like to come?

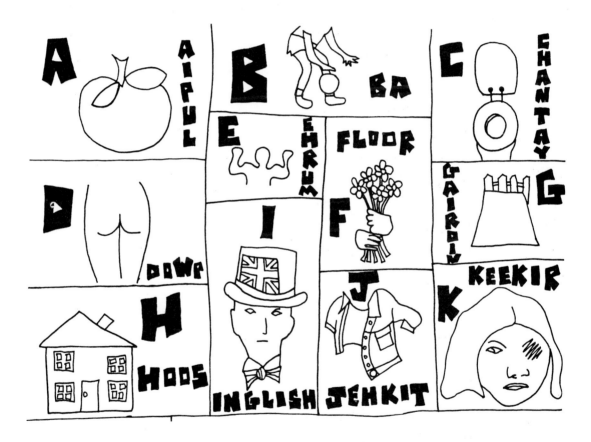

DOCTOR

Tummy upsets and frequent trips to the bathroom can make life a misery, we all know that, but when you're on holiday it's a complete bummer. That is why I have included a section which deals specifically with medical problems.

D. for Dundonian, E. for English.

D. Ull hay ti git a doctir.
E. I need a doctor.

D. Gon git iz a doctir.
E. Would you fetch me a doctor please?

D. Zira doctir aboot?
E. Is there a doctor here?

D. Goanna fone iz a doctir?
E. Please telephone for a doctor.

D. Wharzir a doctir wha speeks inglish?
E. Where is there an English speaking doctor?

PARTS OF THE BODY

Dundonian	English
Ankul	Ankle
Ehrum	Arm
Blud	Blood
Breest	Breast
Chist	Chest
Lug	Ear
Eh	Eye

Fais	Face
Fingir	Finger
Fut	Foot
Haid	Head
Hehrt	Heart
Ja	Jaw
Jiynt	Joint
Lup	Lip
Mooth	Mouth
Mussul	Muscle
Noze	Nose
Shiddir	Shoulder
Theh	Thigh

ILLNESS

Patient . . .

D. Um no affy weel.
E. I'm not feeling well.

D. Um affy no weel.
E. I have a serious complaint.

D. Um sair thair.
E. I have a pain there.

D. Eh feel liyk fehntin.
E. I feel faint/dizzy.

D. Um feelin seek.
E. I'm nauseous.

D. Eh wiz seek.
E. I vomited.

D. Um constipaitit.
E. My bowels have ceased to move.

D. Eh git cald flushiz.
E. I feel shivery.

D. Uv/Eez/Shiz got a/an . . .
E. I've/He/She's got a/an . . .

D.	E.
Biyul	Boil
Dehareeah	Diarrhoea
Constipayshin	Constipation
Piyulz	Haemorrhoids
Cald	Cold
Thi floo	Influenza
A sair behlly	Indigestion
Hoopin cof	Whooping cough

D. 's nuhin bad iz it?
E. It's nothing serious, I hope?

D. Gohnna gee iz a priskripshin?
E. I'd like you to prescribe me some medicine.

D. Um illehrjik ti . . .
E. I'm allergic to . . .

D. Uv bahthir wee mi hehrt.
E. I have a cardiac condition.

D. Um a dehabetik.
E. I'm a diabetic.

D. This iz whut eh iy git.
E. This is my usual medicine.

41

Doctor . . .

D. Whut's thi bahthir?
E. What seems to be the trouble?

D. Wharzit sair?
E. Where does it hurt?

D. Hiz it been sair lang?
E. How long have you had this pain?

D. Tak yir taps aff.
E. Please undress down to the waist.

D. Tak yir breeks an yir drahrz aff.
E. Please remove your trousers and your undergarments.

D. Pit yir sleevz up.
E. Roll up your sleeve.

D. Ull hay ti tak yir blud prehshir.
E. I'm going to take your blood pressure.

D. Huv yi hid this afore?
E. Is this the first time you've had this?

D. Ull tak yir tehmpichir.
E. I'll take your temperature.

D. Opin yir mooth.
E. Open your mouth.

D. Cof.
E. Cough.

D. Big braiths.
E. Breathe deeply.

D. Mehny fagz ir yi on?
E. How many cigarettes do you smoke?

D. Di yi hay a gaid swally?
E. How much alcohol do you drink?

D. Leh doon owir thair.
E. Please lie down over there.

D. Ull gee yi an injehkshin.
E. I will give you an injection.

D. Ull gee yi a priskripshin.
E. I shall prescribe you some medicine.

D. Ull gee yi ahntaybehotik.
E. I'll give you an antibiotic.

D. Snoh bahd.
E. It's nothing to worry about.

OPTICIAN

D. Uv broak mi glehsiz.
E. I've broken my glasses.

D. Kid yi soart thum fir iz?
E. Can you repair them for me?

D. Ull hay ti hay beh foakullz.
E. I require bi-focal glasses.

D. Kin yi cheenj thi lehnziz?
E. Can you change the lenses?

D. Gee iz tints.
E. I would like tinted lenses.

D. How lang diz it tak?
E. When will they be ready?

POPULAR IDIOMS

D. Coors.
E. Of course.

D. Coors no.
E. Of course not.

D. Nay chans.
E. Absolutely not.

D. Yir hayin iz on.
E. You're joking, of course.

D. Nay kiddin.
E. Joking aside.

D. Awa yi go.
E. You're pulling my leg.

D. Nah!
E. Really!

D. Yiron.
E. Agreed.

D. Gon yirsel.
E. Good luck.

D. Hard ti bair.
E. What bad luck.

D. Jist a pehst.
E. What a nuisance.

D. Yi dinna need ti.
E. It's not necessary.

D. It dizna meh'ir.
E. It doesn't matter.

D. 'saffy.
E. How awful.

D. 's brah.
E. It is wonderful.

D. Mair.
E. Encore.

D. Eez a cheekee wee get.
E. He has the cheek of Lucifer.

D. Eh kid tell yi.
E. I'll say.

D. So.
E. I couldn't care less.

D. Eez a but o' a skitso.
E. He is a tough man.

D. Oh meh goad.
E. My goodness.

D. Thank goad.
E. Thank goodness.

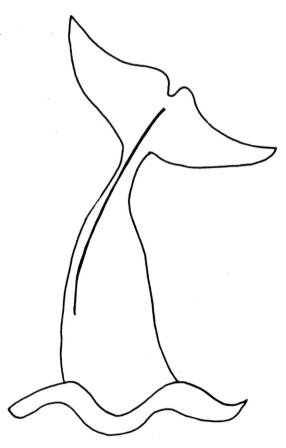

LITTLE BITS AND BOBS OF INFO

NUMBERS

Dundonian	English
Nuhin	0
Ain	1
Twa	2
Three	3
Fowir	4
Fehv	5
Siks	6
Seevin	7
Ait	8
Niyn	9
Ten	10
Illeevin	11
Twehl	12
Thur'een	13
Foar'een	14
Fufteen	15
Siksteen	16
Seevinteen	17
Ai'een	18
Niyn'een	19

Dundonian	English
Twin'ay	20
Thur'ay	30
Fohr'ay	40
Fuftay	50
Sikstay	60
Seevin'ay	70
Ai'ay	80
Niyn'ay	90
A hundir	100

Dundonian	English
Furst	First
Sikind	Second
Thurd	Third
Foarth	Fourth
Fufth	Fifth
Siksth	Sixth
Seevinth	Seventh
Ai'th	Eighth
Niynth	Ninth
Tenth	Tenth
Ains	Once
Twiys	Twice
Haf	Half
A kwahr'ir	A quarter
A thurd	One third

Dundonian	English
A pair o' . . .	A pair of . . .
A dizin	A dozen

DAYS

Day iz it thi day?	What day is today?
Sunday	Sunday
Munday	Monday
Choozday	Tuesday
Widinzday	Wednesday
Thurzday	Thursday
Friyday	Friday
Seh'irday	Saturday
Thi day	Today
Thi moarn	Tomorrow
Yaistirday	Yesterday
Thi day afore . . .	The day before . . .
Thi day eftir . . .	The day after

MONTHS

Janyiray	January
Fehbyiray	February
March	March
Aiprul	April
Miy	May

Dundonian	English
Joon	June
Jileh	July
Ohgist	August
Siptehmbir	September
Uctoabir	October
Nivehmbir	November
Disehmbir	December

A SMALL DICTIONARY OF DUNDONIAN WORDS AND PHRASES

A.

Awan.

English: Go and.

Dundonian sentence: 'Ach awan shufful yoo iy!'

English translation: 'Fiddlesticks, be off with you!'

(This statement is heard from the individual who is at the nucleus of an argument and is quite frustrated at not being able to have his point discussed properly.)

B.

Bizum.

English: Elfish ragamuffin.

Dundonian sentence: 'Aicha cheekee wee bizum yi.'

English translation: 'Hey you impudent little elfish ragamuffin you.'

(This is said to a youngster who has been giving a bit of backchat to an elder of the family or community.)

C.

Chap.

English: Knock.

Dundonian sentence: 'Chap iz up fira berrayz thi moarnz moarnin wull yi?'

English translation: 'Knock me up for the fruit harvesting tomorrow morning, will you?'

(This is only said at selected times of the year, with the exception of signing on days. Usually targeted towards the paperboy, the milkman, or the harvesting overseer.)

D.

Dirlin.

English: Vibrating.

Dundonian sentence: 'Yoo dirlin, orum eh ina car?'

English translation: 'Are you vibrating, for it appears that I am a passenger in a motor vehicle?'

(A sentence such as this is usually pertaining to a leg or foot which belongs to the complainer's partner, e.g, in bed, when the complainer is just about to drift into a comfortable sleep, but is prevented from doing so by the rapid movement of their partner's limb.)

E.

Ehm.

English: I am.

Dundonian sentence: 'Ehm no'n eejit, shirsels'n eejit.'

English translation: 'I am not an idiot, it is yourself who is the idiot.'

(Usually heard at a time of disagreement between the Dundee gentry.)

F.

Fairdeegowk.

English: Witlessly frightened person.

Dundonian sentence: 'Awa yi go, yi big fairdeegowk iy.'

English translation: 'Be off with you, you witlessly frightened person.'

(Often heard when the adult female of the troop, or mithir, as she is better known, asks the pack leader to make sure that the living quarters are secure against night-time intrusion.)

G.

Glaikit.

English: Vacant facial expression.

Dundonian sentence: 'Dinna jist stan air a' thon glaikit wiy, liyk yi dinna ken whut um speekin aboot.'

English translation: 'Don't just stand there wearing a vacant facial expression, as though you know nothing of what I speak.'

(Usually said to a guilty party, who persists in denying their involvement in a dastardly deed.)

H.

Hayvir.

English: A story which is hard to believe./Tall tale.

Dundonian sentence: 'Wanno hayvir yi lehin get.'

English translation: 'Be off with you, and stop telling a story which is hard to believe, you lie-telling bad person.'

(This is heard when the mature female has already heard an explanation from the adult male, about how he managed to get his undergarments the wrong way round, after being at a colonial gathering, which finished half-way through the night.)

I.

Inithirain.

English: Another one.

Dundonian sentence: 'Inithirain! sumpteen yuv hid irridee.'

English translation: 'Another one! you have had quite a lot already.'

J.

Jino.

English: Do you not.

Dundonian sentence: 'Jino eevin ken wha it wiz thit clypt on yi?'

English translation: 'Do you not even know who the person or persons were, who told someone of authority that it was you who did the nasty deed?'

K.

Kreh.

English: Call.

Dundonian sentence: 'Dinna yoo kreh me diytit, yi nyaff yi.'

English translation: 'I wish you would kindly refrain from calling me completely hopeless, you person of insufficient status.'

(Phrases such as this are only heard in Council meetings. Commoners do not usually hear such vileties of the vocal chords.)

L.

Loabee.

English: Hallway.

Dundonian sentence: 'Saboot tıym yi pehntit thi loabee zitno?'

English translation: 'It is about time you painted the hallway, is it not?'

(This is said to the adult male Dundonian on close inspection of the present decorative condition of the interior of the hovelhold, bringing it to his attention that the hallway is in dire need of a bit of D.I.Y. handymanship.)

M.

Mingin.

English: The fragrance of a sewage worker.

Dundonian sentence: 'At manky towragz mingin!'

English translation: 'That unclean person of ill-repute has the fragrance of a sewage worker!'

(This is a statement usually muttered, or whispered, concerning the aroma which has just infiltrated the environment. e.g, bus, bus queue, post office queue, or any place where undesirables may lurk.)

N.

Nyaff.

English: Person of insufficient status.

Dundonian sentence: 'Needna bahthir aboot at nyaff, eez no thi ful shullin.'

English translation: 'You need not bother about that person of insufficient status, for he is two sandwiches short of a picnic, in the upstairs department.'

(Usually said to a raging Dundonian in an attempt to curb his temper towards another, pointing out that he has more sense than his counterpart.)

O.

Owir.

English: Over.

Dundonian sentence: 'Ats owir thi tap zitno?'

English translation: 'That is over your personal requirement is it not?'

(Sometimes said by the harvesting overseer when he sees his slaves carrying three or more, large buckets of raspberries on to the 'Berry bus'.)

P.

Pletty.

English: Walkway. (Commonly found on old tenement buildings.)

Dundonian sentence: 'Airz ald Anny hingin owira pletty.'

English translation: 'There is the elderly woman Ann, leaning over the barrier surrounding the tenement walkway.'

Q.

Sadly, the letter Q no longer exists in the Dundonian vocabulary. It has been substituted by the letters K or C.

R.

Ruft.

English: Upward eruption of excess body gasses.

Dundonian sentence: 'Joo ruft air?'

English translation: 'Was that you partaking in an upward eruption of excess body gases a moment ago?'

S.

Slabirin.

English: Carelessly spilling.

Dundonian sentence: 'Wacha skunnir, yir slabirin.'

English translation: 'Look out, you uncoordinated person, you are carelessly spilling.'

(Sometimes said to a drunk, when he appears to be carelessly spilling his drink onto unsuspecting strangers, out of his mouth whilst in mid-drunken babble.)

T.

Tappy.

English: Container lid.

Dundonian sentence: 'Pit thi tappy ona joog eftir yi.'

English translation: 'Kindly put the container lid back on the jug once you have finished.'

(This is a statement normally used in the training of the young Dundonian, whereby he or she, learns to replace things after use.)

U.

Uv.

English: I have.

Dundonian sentence: 'Uv gota wahnt aboot iz, 'na dah ken whut it iz.'

English translation: 'I have an exceedingly strange craving lurking about my person and I am unable to isolate it.'

(This is usually said to the subject's partner, or close friend, in the evening when boredom sets in, not unlike rigor mortis.)

W.

Watna.

English: Do you want a . . .

Dundonian sentence: 'Watna but pink lint on yir peece?'

English translation: 'Do you want a piece of cold meat on your sandwich?'

(This famous Dundee phrase is heard when the adult female asks the adult male about the requirements of his luncheon habits. The luncheon is usually prepared in the home and taken to the male's place of work by means of a 'Peece poke'.)

X.

X.

English: Alexander is./Alexander's.

Dundonian sentence: 'X a nuttir zee no.'

English translation: This saying has two meanings. Firstly, it can be taken as 'Alexander is quick witted and a very jolly fellow.' Or it can also mean that Alexander is not the type of chap which you would like your sister to associate with.

Y.

Yir.

English: Your/You are.

Dundonian sentence: 'Yir oota windee pawl.'

English translation: This simply means that the subject has no chance in succeeding with his or her task.

Z.

Zatno.

English: Is that not.

Dundonian sentence: 'Zatno Ehrchay ona pugee.'

English translation: 'Is that not our good friend Archibald investing in the communal games and recreation machine.'

(This is only heard in the adult meeting hall, otherwise known as 'thi boozir'.)

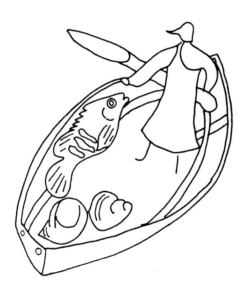

SPOT THE DIFFERENCE

In this section, I shall endeavour to explain the fundamental differences of certain words and phrases which are of great importance, especially if you want to be able to express yourself in the context in which it is intended.

What's the difference between . . . ?

A 'Chucky', and a 'Dockay'.

A 'Chucky', is a small stone, which is thrown in an attempt to gain someone's attention. For example, if a friend is sleeping late and won't answer the doorbell, a 'Chucky', is usually thrown at the bedroom window to rouse them. A 'Dockay', however, is a much larger stone, and if thrown, it is usually intended to cause actual bodily harm. In brief, a 'Chucky', is used to wake from sleep, and a 'Dockay' is used to put to sleep.

'Haid thi ba', and 'Stot thi ba'.

'Haid thi ba', is a friendly term for a relative, or acquaintance, who is younger than yourself. In a sense it is a patronising term, but put into the proper context, it can be user-friendly. 'Stot thi ba' is definitely not user-friendly. It is a term used to describe an adult who has a romantic incline towards someone who is a great deal younger than themselves.

'Clortay', and 'Barkit'.

'Clortay', in itself, means dirty, grimy, or grubby. It is an honest word describing honest dirt. Dirt which has only recently accumulated. 'Barkit', on the other hand, describes dirt or grime which, for some unforeseen reason, has been allowed to become ingrained.

'No affy weel' and 'Affy no weel'.

'No affy weel' and 'Affy no weel', are both terms used to describe one's physical or mental condition. 'No affy weel' is a condition in which the sufferer has a minor complaint, such as a cold, an ache, a pain, or a general feeling of being unwell. In contrast, 'Affy no weel', is a much more serious complaint. People who complain of being 'Affy no weel' are either hypochondriacs, or very unlucky people indeed.

'Bowfin', and 'Bogin'.

'Bowfin' is a word which describes something, or someone with an unsavoury odour. It doesn't just mean smelly in the conventional sense, it is an odour of exceedingly rotten proportions. It is often used to describe body odours like feet and armpits. 'Bogin' is a word which describes something which is both dirty and smelly e.g. a toilet, a drain, a tramp, etc.

'Fir thi haid', and 'Aff thir haid'.

The difference between 'Fir thi haid', and 'Aff thir haid', is simple. 'Fir thi haid' is a term used when playing ball games, especially football. It is a command which is shouted to a

65

team-mate, emphasising your request for the ball to be pitched up high, so as it can be played by your head. 'Aff thir haid' however, is not in any way connected with ball games. It is a term used to describe a person's mentality, ranging from being light-hearted and silly, to being an outright hospital case.

'Haf pan' and 'Pan loafay'.

Although these two sayings sound alike, their meanings are as far apart as the north and south poles. 'Haf pan' is the local term used for a loaf of bread. There are two main types of bread sold in Dundee, plain bread and pan bread. The latter is commonly known as a 'Haf pan'. 'Pan loafay', on the other hand, is a term used to describe a Dundonian voice which has a considerable English influence. 'Pan loafay' is usually spoken by the migrant Dundonians who have somehow managed to escape the schemes, by either buying their own bungalow, or renting a bungalow. Either way, they are people of a working-class origin who are frustrated at not quite being middle-class.

'Snottir' and 'Doolee'.

N.B. The difference between 'Snottirz' and 'Dooleez' might cause offence to some readers. So if you are one of those people who don't like facing humanistic facts, you'd better skip this one.

You've probably heard the age old saying, 'What came first, the chicken or the egg?' A similar saying has puzzled Dundonians for many years. 'Whut cum furst, a snottir or a doolee?' I think that it is about time this was clarified. First, let us take the 'Snottir'. A 'Snottir', to put it bluntly, is nasal mucus. It is the slimy, sticky, sort of mucus which requires the use of a handkerchief to assist in its extraction. 'Snottirz' cannot be picked, they must be blown out of the nose with extreme force. Whereas a 'Doolee', which is also nasal mucus, must be picked, a 'Doolee' is a versatile type of mucus which can be picked, rolled, squashed and flicked with comparative ease. As for the question 'What came first . . . ?' All I can say is, who cares, as long as there's not one stuck to my cheek.

'Stot' and 'Stottir'.

To 'Stot' is to bounce. For example, you may 'Stot' a ball on the ground, or if you are unlucky enough to be in a traffic accident, you might 'Stot' your head against the windscreen. If, by chance, a native Dundonian was to say to you, 'Ehll stot yoor haid riyt aff that wah', your best course of action would be to run. And make it fast. Whatever you do, don't pull out your phrase book for assistance or you might find yourself wearing it. You may well think that a 'Stottir' is a person who 'Stots' things. If you do, you're wrong. A 'Stottir' is someone or something of extreme excellence.

'Mi broo' and 'Thi broo'.

'Mi broo' is a term used for describing your forehead. You can use it for saying things like, 'Uv got a plook on mi broo' or, 'Is that a skahb on mi broo . . . ?' 'Thi broo', however, is something totally different. 'Thi broo' is the colloquial term for the unemployment benefit office, or dole. Take care not to get muddled up between 'Mi broo' and 'Thi broo', especially if you are unemployed, or you might end up signing your name on your own forehead.

'*Keek*' *and* '*Keekir*'.

'Keek' is a great word. It means simply, glance. This word is used in a variety of ways. Such as, having a 'Keek' in the oven, to check on the Sunday roast, or having a 'Keek' out the window to see who is at the front door. It is used frequently when in the company of small children, especially when playing games such as 'Keek-a-bow' or peek-a-boo, as the English call it. 'Keekir,' on the other hand, is a more serious word. It is widely used in Scotland as a whole, and more often in Boxing rings. A 'Keekir' is a black eye.

NOW TO TEST YOUR TRANSLATION ABILITY

First, let us translate a poem.

> Thir wiz an ald man caad Scobie
> Wha livd in a hoos in thi Stobie
> Eez wiyf caad Ann
> Yaizd shiz gaid frehin pan
> Ti belt shiz spouse riyt in thi loabee.

And now the translation.

The poem is a tale of a wife exercising her matrimonial rights, by heavily chastising her man for his inconsideration and blatant absenteeism from the nuptial resting place.

Now it is your turn to translate.

Translate the following excerpts from *Diary of an Unknown Whaler.*

It is a sad fact that the original text of the diary was destroyed in a fire. But as luck would have it, the unknown whaler's grand-daughter, on his wife's side, had the good fortune to possess a photographic memory and was therefore able to obtain reprints from Boots photographic department, at an undisclosed price.

The diary, in all its splendour, reads as follows:

Thurzday, 6th Disembir 1883.
Deer dehray,

Went on thi Fiyfee thi day wee Wattie. Nivir agehn! Thi thing iz, eez went an took a fansy ti thi lassie wha selz thi tickits. So mugginz me hid ti sit aboot liyk a feechee peece at a picnic fir fehv crossinz o' the Tiy, whiyul Wattie chansiz eez hand. 'Fansy a wak roond thi cattle merkit when yuv feenisht yir shuft?' saiz Wattie. Yi shood'uv herd ir! Man, did

69

shi no jist go spair. Pit Wattie riyt in eez plais shi did. 'Lassies fay meh end o' thi toon dinna wak roond nay cattle merkit.' shi saiz. 'We hay waks doon beh Magdullin Green.' Eh jist coodna stand beh an watch Wattie beein tokt doon ti liyk that, spehshully fay a wummin kinductir. So eh went an stood it thi back o' thi boat an mindid mi ain bizniss. That's when eh seen it. A huge Humfy-backit whale, wee a tail thi sez o' thi provist's hoos, an a noze liyk eh dinna ken whut. Thir wiz a fyoo wee rowin boats skootin aboot, trehin ti catch it. Eh eevin saw sum bairnz chuckin stainz at it. Thi tickit lassie stood ah thon smug wiy an saiz ti Wattie, 'If yi catch iz that whale, ull think aboot gayin ti a pehrtay wee yi on hugminay.' Pair Wattie, eh think eez gone saft. 'Nay bahthir darlin' ee went an saiz ti ir.

Friyday, 7th Disembir 1883.
Deer dehray,
   Yull nivir gais! Wattie's went an harpoond thi Humfy-backit whale! Ah thay so calld priffehshinul whalirz, wee ah thir ropes an gunz coodna day it, but Wattie did. Well ee didna igzactly harpoon thi whale. Ee yaizd a gairdin fork, but thi iffect wiz thi same. Well neerly thi same. Thi whale didna akchully deh tho. Pair craitir. It must be murdir huvin ti sweem aboot thi rivir wee a gairdin fork stuk in yir ehrs. Eh widna be sirprehzd if Wattie got eez naim in thi paipir fir it tho.
   P.S. Eh neerly bot a nyoo shirt thi day, but eh disiydid agenst it, cuz ull nay doot git ain fir mi krissmiss fay sumbidee.

Choozday, 1st Janyiwary 1884.
Deer dehray,
   A happy nyoo yeer, a bottul o' beer, an a skelp in thi lug tull nikst nyoo yeer! Last niyts pehrtay wiz thi gehm! Um stull haf schood. Wattie went an maid a fail o' eezsel eftir ee wiz duft beh thi lassie wha selz thi tickits on thi Fiyfee. 'Shi iridee telt yi Wattie man. Nay whale, nay chans', eh saiz ti um. 'Jist firgit ir. Shiz affy much on thi toffay nozd siyd enywiy.' Bit

71

thirz nay tellin a man whaz bissotid beh a wummin in uniform. Wha kenz whut ee miyt day nikst.

Nyoo yeerz rezulyooshin—Dinna start sumhin yi miyt rigret eftir.

Friyday, 4th Janyiwary 1884.
Deer dehray,

Fowir dayz inti thi nyoo yeer an uv irridee broke mi nyoo yeerz rezulyooshin. Um stuck in a wee rowin boat, twin'ay oad miyulz aff thi coast o' Montrose. Wattie pirswaydid iz ti help um catch thi whale. 'Whut if it keeps sweemin an wi end up awa doon beh China?' Eh saiz ti Wattie. An ee caim strait back wee, 'Then wull jist hay ti hay sweet an soor whale blubbir fir wir tee.' Eez sum boy iz Wattie. Wi wirna oot in thi wahtir beh wirselz. Thir wiz loadz o' ithir wee boats hingin aboot tay. It wiz thi whale thit eh fehlt sorry fir. Iviree tiym it cum ti thi surfis fir air, it wiz pehltit wee a big load o' harpoonz. An iviree tiym it swum awa deep, it wiz pehltit wee a big load o' abuse.

Munday, 7th Janyiwary 1884.
Deer dehray,

Whut a day! Um buggird! Thi whalez been cot it last. No beh me an Wattie tho. Ulltho it wizna wee thi lak o' trehin, eh kid tell yi. Mi harpoonin ehrum feelz liyk it's aboot ti drap aff. If thirz wun thing thit eh kid day wee, it's mi ain bed. Strainj trip this hiz been. Uv lehrind a lot aboot Wattie thit eh nivir reeullehzd afore. Jist wee hingz, liyk thi wiy eez noze ringkulz up when ee greets eez wiy ti sleep. Or, thi wiy eez earz jump up an doon when ee blahz eez noze. Eh think Wattie's glehd thit thi whale hunt's feenisht tay. 'Yi dinna beh eny chans ken thi naim o' thi raid haird lassie wha wurks on thi tripe coontir it Ogulvy's thi boochir di yi?' ee saiz ti iz, iz wi sat in wir wee boat, watchin thi priffehshinul whalirz towin awa thir Humfy-backit whale.

P.S. Uv jist miyndid sumhin. Oh buggir it, uv firgot whut it wiz.

Yet another exercise

This exercise, bristling with morals, is a children's bed-time story. There are many variations. Here is the original:

Now thi gaffir lahd o' ah thi gairdin centir wiz a fella caad Toad. Ee wiz thi Laird o' ah thi land. Ee wiz a fair inuf lahd, but a reel stiklir fir dayin hingz beh thi book. Noo thi Laird wiz nay man fir slahkin, infakt ee wiz a riyt graftir. Ee wehnt an plantit ah soarts o' hingz in thi gairdin centir. Floorz, booshiz, an klondiyks o' difrint kiyndz o' froot treez. In thi middul o' thi gairdin centir ee plantit eez twa faivrits. An aipul tree, an inithir aipul tree. Man, did thay treez jist no git spiyulld. Treetid thum liyk bairnz ee did. Enywiy, eftir a whiylee thi Laird got a but fed-up wee huvin ti day ah thi gairdinin eezsel, so ee wehnt an took on a ful-tiym gairdinir caad Angus.

'Thirz a cupul o' hingz eh wàhnt made cleer afore yi start wurkin heer Angus,' sais thi Laird. 'Eh dinna miynd yi takin thi oad but o' froot haim wee yi, but see thon twa treez owir thair,' saiz thi Laird piyntin oot eez twa faivirits. 'If yi pinsh eny o' thi aipulz fay them, yull be sehkt on thi spot.'

So wee jist a verbal contract, Angus sehts aboot eez nyoo joab. It furst, it seemd liyk a brah cooshee joab ti Angus. But beh thi tiym thi summir wiz in ful sweeng, Angus wiz it thi end o' eez tehthir wee thi hyooj amount o' wurk thit thir wiz ti day. So ee lehgd it up ti see thi Laird, an telt um thit ee jist coodna cope wee ah thi gairdinin eezsel, an wiz it no aboot tiym thit thi Laird took on an ekstra pair o' hanz.

Liyk eh saiz afore, thi Laird wiz a fair inuf lahd. So ee saiz ti Angus,

'Hiz that wee wiyf o' yoorz no manijd ti git irsel a wee joabee yit?'

'Nut,' saiz Angus, 'Bit shiz awa trehn fir ain this eftirnain.'

'Whut ti day,' thi Laird saiz ti Angus, 'is ti nip haim jisnoo, an catch yir missus afore shi laivz thi hoos. Tell thi lassie thit yuv been maid up ti haid gairdinir, an if shi wahnts shi kid hay a wee joabee in thi gairdin centir. Pert-tiym yi undirstand.'

Well, Angus wiz maid up. Ee behltit haim an telt eez wiyf.
Ir naim beh thi wiy, wiz Ena. As tiym wehnt on, Ena bicaim
a dab-hand it thi gairdinin gehm. Shi dun ah soarts o' joabz.
Plantin, weedin, dayin thi books, seein ti thi custimirz, thi list
wiz endliss. Angus an Ena wurkt awa thigithir nay bahthir.
Liyf in thi gairdin centir wiz brah, tull ai day, in wahkt thi
haid lahd o' thi froot shop doon thi road. Ee wiz a riyt fleh-
man, thit wehnt beh thi naim o' Jake thi snake. Ee turnt on
thi pah'ir as sain as ee saw Ena.

'Howz mi wee darlin thi day?' ee askt Ena, in ain o' them
moochin voices.

'If meh man wiz ti wahk in thi door riyt now an catch yoo
speekin ti me liyk that, eed brak yir nehk!' saiz Ena, as politely
meeninful as shi cood undir thi sircumstansiz.

'Nay sweht doll,' saiz Jake. 'Snoh yoo thit um eftir enywiy,
its yir froot an vej.'

Jake plaist an oardir fir fehv sehks o' tatties an fowir boksiz
o' timah'iz, then turnt on thi fleh-man pah'ir.

'Di yooz ivir git ti tak eny o' yir froot haim wee yi?'

'Oh eh!' saiz Ena. 'Wi git ti tak iz much iz wi wahnt. Iksept
wir no alood ti tak eny aipulz fay thay twa treez owir thondir.'
shi saiz, pointin oot thi Lairdz twa faivirit treez.

Well it didna tak lang tull Jake thi fleh-man snake, hid
pirswaidit Ena ti hay a wee pochul goin wee ah thi froot thit
hur an ir man git fir free. As thi nikst fyoo weeks wehnt beh,
greed hid got thi beh'ir o' Jake. Ee wahntit mair an mair froot
an vej on thi siyd fay Ena an Angus.

'Whut aboot thon aipul treez?' Jake saiz ti Ena. 'Thir
hingin wee aipulz. Kid yi no sneek a cupul o' boksiz o' thir
oot tay?'

'Nay chans,' saiz Ena, 'Eh telt yi afore. Wir no alood ti tak
thay aipulz.'

'Pit it this wiy,' saiz Jake, 'If yi dinna gee iz a cupul o'
boksiz o' thon aipulz, um gohnna tell yir gaffir thit yuv been
fidlin.'

Ena wiz shattird. 'Ahriyt,' shi saiz, 'ull gee yi twa boksiz this
tiym, but that's it! Yull git nay mair oot thi back door fay us!'

That eftirnain, Angus herd thi Laird hayin a wee dandir
throo thi gairdin centir.

75

'Whut's this!' shoutid thi Laird. 'Whaz been dobeein mi aipulz?'

Thir wiz nuhin Angus an Ena kid say in thir ain difehns. Thi Laird wehnt an sehkt thum on thi spot. Jist liyk ee saiz ee wid.

'Yiz kid tak yir peece pokes an git ti buggiree,' saiz thi Laird. 'An dinna bahthir askin fir nay rehfrins.'

Wee that, Angus an Ena wir flung oot thi gairdin centir, an Jake thi snake got thi polis sehnt ti eez door ti ricuvir thi Lairdz aipulz.

WURDZ AN MEENINZ

D. for Dundonian, E. for English.

A

D. Abdee.......................... E. Everybody.

D. Aboot.......................... E. About.

D. Aff............................. E. Off.

D. Affy........................... E. Awful.

D. Aicha! .... E. Hey you!

D. Ains .... E. Once.

D. Aipul.......................... E. Apple.

D. Air............................ E. There.

D. Alain .... E. Alone.

D. Alang .... E. Along.

D. Ald .... E. Old.

D. Argee .... E. Argue.

D. Atween........................ E. Between.

D. Awa .... E. Go.

B

D. Ba............................. E. Ball.

D. Bahthir .... E. Bother.

D. Baird.......................... E. Beard.

D. Bairnz .... E. Children.

D. Baist.......................... E. Beast, animal.

D. Bait........................... E. Boot.

D. Barkit.......................... **E.** Very dirty.

D. Beh............................ **E.** By/Buy.

D. Biyd........................... **E.** Stay.

D. Biyul......................... **E.** A boil, infected swelling.

D. Blah......................... **E.** Blow.

D. Blehthir..................... **E.** Talk foolishly, a lie.

D. Blud.......................... **E.** Blood.

D. Boadee....................... **E.** Body.

D. Boak......................... **E.** Retch, vomit.

D. Bogin........................ **E.** Very dirty, smelly.

D. Boray........................ **E.** Borrow.

D. Bowfin...................... **E.** Smelly, dirty.

D. Brah......................... **E.** Very good, fine.

D. Braith....................... **E.** Breath.

D. Brak......................... **E.** Break.

D. Breeks...................... **E.** Trousers.

D. Breest...................... **E.** Breast.

D. Brithir..................... **E.** Brother.

D. Broo......................... **E.** The forehead

D. Broo......................... **E.** Unemployment benefit office.

D. Burul........................ **E.** Revolve quickly, spin.

D. But .... **E.** Bit.

C

D. Cald......................... **E.** Cold.

D. Canna....................... **E.** Cannot.

D. Cannul...................... **E.** Candle.

D. Canny .... **E.** Gentle/gently.

D. Cha .... **E.** Chew.

D. Chaip .... **E.** Cheap.

D. Chait .... **E.** Cheat.

D. Chantay .... **E.** A chamber pot, toilet.

D. Chap .... **E.** A knock, blow.

D. Cheenj .... **E.** Change.

D. Chist .... **E.** Chest.

D. Chuck .... **E.** Throw.

D. Chucky .... **E.** A small stone.

D. Cla .... **E.** Claw, scratch.

D. Claiz .... **E.** Clothes.

D. Cleek .... **E.** Association, secretive group.

D. Clivir .... **E.** Clever.

D. Cloot .... **E.** A piece of cloth rag.

D. Clortay .... **E.** Dirty.

D. Clo'say .... **E.** Tenement building.

D. Cludgee .... **E.** Outhouse, toilet.

D. Clypt .... **E.** Informed. (Against.)

D. Cooard .... **E.** Coward.

D. Coont .... **E.** Count.

D. Coors .... **E.** Coarse, rough.

D. Cooshee .... **E.** Easy.

D. Cowp .... **E.** Tip.

D. Crabbit .... **E.** Bad tempered.

D. Crappir........................ **E.** Coward.

D. Cundee........................ **E.** Roadside drain.

D

D. Daif .... **E.** Deaf.

D. Daith........................ **E.** Death.

D. Dandir........................ **E.** Stroll, saunter.

D. Dehmind .... **E.** Diamond.

D. Dehnir........................ **E.** Dinner.

D. Dehray .... **E.** Diary.

D. Didna........................ **E.** Didn't.

D. Dinna........................ **E.** Don't.

D. Diytit .... **E.** Stupid.

D. Dockay...................... **E.** A large stone.

D. Doo........................... **E.** Pigeon.

D. Dooch .... **E.** Hit/Bump. (Impact.)

D. Dook........................ **E.** Duck, into water.

D. Doolee........................ **E.** Hardened nasal mucus.

D. Doon........................ **E.** Down.

D. Doot .... **E.** Doubt.

D. Dowp .... **E.** The buttocks.

D. Drahrz........................ **E.** Underwear.

D. Drap .... **E.** Drop.

D. Dreep........................ **E.** Drip.

D. Drehv........................ **E.** Drive.

D. Droond...................... **E.** Drowned.

D. Dub .... **E.** Puddle.

D. Dunt .... **E.** Bump, knock.

E

D. Eejit........................... **E.** Idiot.

D. Eevin .... **E.** Even.

D. Eez .... **E.** His/he is.

D. Eftir.......................... **E.** After.

D. Eh .... **E.** Eye.

D. Eh .... **E.** I.

D. Eh .... **E.** Yes.

D. Ehrum........................ **E.** Arm.

D. Ehrs .... **E.** The arse.

F

D. Fa .... **E.** Fall.

D. Faird .... **E.** Frightened.

D. Fais............................ **E.** Face.

D. Fay .... **E.** From.

D. Feechee .... **E.** Horrible. (Sickly.)

D. Feenish........................ **E.** Finish.

D. Fehnt .... **E.** Faint.

D. Fehst.......................... **E.** Fast.

D. Fehv........................... **E.** Five.

D. Fingir .... **E.** Finger.

D. Fir .... E. For.

D. Firbeh .... E. Except.

D. Flair .... E. Floor.

D. Fleein .... E. Very drunk.

D. Fleg....................... E. Fright.

D. Floor .... E. Flower, flour

D. Foond..................... E. Found.

D. Foostee................... E. Stale.

D. Footir.................... E. Fidget.

D. Forkay Taylay .... E. An earwig.

D. Fowir .... E. Four.

D. Fowk...................... E. Folk.

D. Freend................... E. Friend, relative.

D. Freh .... E. Fry.

D. Ful...................... E. Full.

D. Fund .... E. Found.

D. Fut...................... E. Foot.

G

D. Gaird .... E. Guard.

D. Gairdin................... E. Garden.

D. Gais .... E. Guess.

D. Geez .... E. Give me.

D. Gehm.................... E. Game.

D. Gehthir .... E. Gather.

D. Get .... E. Bad person.

D. Girn............................ E. Winge, whimper.

D. Git.............................. E. Get.

D. Glaikit......................... E. Foolish, stupid, thoughtless.

D. Glehd.......................... E. Glad.

D. Glehsiz........................ E. Glasses.

D. Gochul .... E. Spit.

D. Goosee .... E. A segment of fruit.

D. Gowk .... E. Silly person.

D. Greet .... E. Cry.

D. Grund .... E. Ground.

D. Gutirz .... E. Mud, muddy puddles.

H

D. Haid .... E. Head.

D. Haik............................ E. Scrounge.

D. Hail .... E. Whole.

D. Haim........................... E. Home.

D. Hakit .... E. Ugly.

D. Halakit........................ E. Clumsy.

D. Hay............................. E. Have.

D. Hayvir......................... E. Speak nonsense, a lie.

D. Heelee .... E. Thick crusted slice of bread.

D. Hehrm......................... E. Harm.

D. Hehrt .... E. Heart.

D. Hid.............................. **E.** Had.

D. Hing .... **E.** Thing.

D. Hing .... **E.** Hang.

D. Hiya............................ **E.** Hello.

D. Hoos .... **E.** House.

D. Howk .... **E.** Pick.

D. Hud .... **E.** Hold.

D. Huv .... **E.** Have.

D. Huvna .... **E.** Have not.

I

D. Ichay-coo .... **E.** Prickly seeds of the dog rose.

D. Inglish .... **E.** English.

D. Inti .... **E.** Into

D. Irridee .... **E.** Already.

D. Ivree .... **E.** Every.

D. Iy................................ **E.** Eh!

D. Iz................................ **E.** Me.

D. Izna .... **E.** Is not.

J

D. Ja................................ **E.** Jaw.

D. Jag .... **E.** Prick, pierce.

D. Janay........................... **E.** Janitor.

D. Jaykay .... **E.** Alcoholic.

D. Jehkit .... **E.** Jacket.

D. Jino .... **E.** Do you not.

D. Jisnoo .... **E.** Just now.

D. Jiynt .... **E.** Joint.

D. Joab .... **E.** Job.

D. Joog .... **E.** Jug.

D. Joogul......................... **E.** Agitate.

D. Jook .... **E.** Jersey, jacket, tunic.

K

D. Kail............................ **E.** Home-made vegetable soup.

D. Keech......................... **E.** Excrement.

D. Keek .... **E.** Peep, glance.

D. Keekir .... **E.** A black eye.

D. Ken........................... **E.** Know.

D. Kent........................... **E.** Knew.

D. Kid .... **E.** Could.

D. Kreh.......................... **E.** Call.

L

D. La .... **E.** Law.

D. Laft........................... **E.** Loft, attic.

D. Laid .... **E.** Lead, the metal.

D. Laiv .... **E.** Leave.

D. Lang.......................... **E.** Long.

D. Lahray........................ E. Lorry.

D. Lavee .... E. Toilet.

D. Lehdir .... E. Ladder.

D. Lehin .... E. Lying.

D. Lehrind .... E. Learnt.

D. Len .... E. Loan.

D. Loabee........................ E. Hallway.

D. Luft .... E. Lift.

D. Lug .... E. Ear.

D. Lum .... E. Chimney.

D. Lup .... E. Lip.

M

D. Mair........................... E. More.

D. Maist.......................... E. Most.

D. Mak .... E. Make.

D. Manky........................ E. Filthy.

D. Mapit .... E. Thick headed, stupid.

D. Maskin .... E. Infusing. (Tea.)

D. Meenistir .... E. Minister.

D. Meenit........................ E. Minute.

D. Meh .... E. My.

D. Mehtirs....................... E. Matters.

D. Mi .... E. My.

D. Mink.......................... E. A ragamuffin, poor person.

D. Misel............................ **E.** Myself.

D. Miyndid........................ **E.** Remembered.

D. Mooth .... **E.** Mouth.

D. Moaruz moarnin .... **E.** Tomorrow morning.

D. Mussul........................ **E.** Muscle.

N

D. Nab.............................. **E.** Catch, grab.

D. Nablir.......................... **E.** Experienced fruit picker.

D. Naikit.......................... **E.** Naked.

D. Naim........................... **E.** Name.

D. Nain............................ **E.** None.

D. Nait .... **E.** Neat.

D. Nat .... **E.** And that.

D. Nathin......................... **E.** And everything.

D. Nay............................. **E.** None.

D. Neebir........................ **E.** Neighbour.

D. Needna........................ **E.** Need not.

D. Neep .... **E.** Turnip.

D. Nehray .... **E.** Narrow.

D. Nikst........................... **E.** Next.

D. Nivir .... **E.** Never.

D. Nivreehin .... **E.** And everything.

D. No .... **E.** Not.

D. Nut............................. **E.** No.

O

D. Oor .... **E.** Our.

D. Oor .... **E.** An hour.

D. Oot .... **E.** Out.

D. Oray .... **E.** Ordinary/common. (Talk.)

D. Orum .... **E.** Or I am.

D. Owir .... **E.** Over.

D. Oxtir......................... **E.** The armpit.

P

D. Paipir .... **E.** Paper.

D. Pais........................... **E.** Peace.

D. Palay .... **E.** Friendly.

D. Pan .... **E.** Pawn.

D. Payvee........................ **E.** Pavement.

D. Peece......................... **E.** Sandwich.

D. Peen.......................... **E.** Pin.

D. Peetee .... **E.** Pity.

D. Peh .... **E.** Pie.

D. Pehnday...................... **E.** An arched walkway.

D. Pehntit .... **E.** Painted.

D. Pehrt......................... **E.** Part.

D. Pehrtay....................... **E.** Party.

D. Pirnikitay.................... **E.** Fussy, very precise.

D. Plais .... **E.** Place.

D. Plait .... **E.** Plate.

D. Plook........................... **E.** Pimple.

D. Plunk .... **E.** Play truant.

D. Poke........................... **E.** Paper bag.

D. Poodir .... **E.** Powder.

D. Poolee .... **E.** Indoor washing line.

D. Poond......................... **E.** A pound, money.

D. Poor .... **E.** Pour.

D. Press .... **E.** Cupboard.

D. Pugee .... **E.** Fruit machine.

D. Pund .... **E.** A pound, weight.

D. Pus............................. **E.** Face. (Slang.)

D. Pyuchy .... **E.** Horrible/sickly.

R

D. Rah.............................. **E.** Raw.

D. Raidir......................... **E.** Blush, a red face.

D. Raik .... **E.** Sift through, look for something.

D. Rang .... **E.** Wrong.

D. Rank .... **E.** Not very good.

D. Rinaig......................... **E.** Refuse responsibility, shirk.

D. Ringin .... **E.** Soaked, especially from rain.

D. Roond .... **E.** Round.

D. Roostee .... **E.** Rusty.

D. Ruft .... **E.** Burp.

S

D. Sa .... **E.** A saw, to saw.

D. Saboot .... **E.** It is about.

D. Saft .... **E.** Soft.

D. Sair .... **E.** Sore.

D. Sait .... **E.** Seat.

D. Sannayz .... **E.** Plimsoles.

D. Sap .... **E.** A soft, weak-willed person.

D. Sat? .... **E.** What is that?

D. Sat .... **E.** Salt.

D. Scaffay .... **E.** Refuse collector.

D. Scoot .... **E.** Squirt.

D. Seek .... **E.** Sick.

D. Seevin .... **E.** Seven.

D. Sez .... **E.** Size.

D. Shair .... **E.** Sure.

D. Shak .... **E.** Shake.

D. Shakaydoon .... **E.** Makeshift bed.

D. Shiddir .... **E.** Shoulder.

D. Shirsel .... **E.** It is yourself.

D. Shiz .... **E.** She has.

D. Skail .... **E.** School.

D. Skeh............................ **E.** Sky.

D. Skek............................ **E.** Glance, look at.

D. Skel............................ **E.** Spill.

D. Skelp........................... **E.** Slap/Hit.

D. Skittir .... **E.** Diarrhoea.

D. Skoosh........................ **E.** Gush in squirts, splash.

D. Skoosh........................ **E.** Lemonade.

D. Slaivir......................... **E.** Saliva.

D. Sleekit .... **E.** Sneaky.

D. Smeg .... **E.** Nasal mucus.

D. Smert .... **E.** Smart.

D. Snah............................ **E.** Snow.

D. Snect.......................... **E.** Locked.

D. Soart .... **E.** Mend/repair.

D. Soond......................... **E.** Sound.

D. Soor .... **E.** Sour.

D. Sosh .... **E.** Co-operative society shop.

D. Spiyul......................... **E.** Spoil.

D. Sput .... **E.** Spat.

D. Spyugee .... **E.** A sparrow.

D. Stain .... **E.** Stone.

D. Stannin....................... **E.** Standing.

D. Stoor .... **E.** Dust.

D. Stot............................ **E.** Bounce.

D. Sumhin....................... **E.** Something.

D. Swally .... **E.** Swallow.

D. Sweem .... **E.** Swim.

D. Sweeng .... **E.** Swing.

D. Syne oot .... **E.** Rinse out.

T

D. Tak .... **E.** Take.

D. Tap .... **E.** Top.

D. Tay .... **E.** Toe.

D. Theh .... **E.** Thigh.

D. Thi .... **E.** The.

D. Thit .... **E.** That.

D. Threed .... **E.** Thread.

D. Tiy .... **E.** The River Tay.

D. Toaly .... **E.** Excrement.

D. Toffay nozd .... **E.** Snobbish.

D. Trachul .... **E.** Walk wearily, bedraggle.

D. Tully .... **E.** Evening paper.

D. Twa .... **E.** Two.

U

D. Ull .... **E.** I will.

D. Um .... **E.** I am.

D. Umpteen .... **E.** Several.

D. Uv .... **E.** I have.

W

D.	E.
D. Wah	E. Wall.
D. Wak	E. Walk.
D. Wan	E. Go away and . . .
D. Wee	E. Small.
D. Weel	E. Well.
D. Weeng	E. Wing.
D. Weesht	E. Quiet.
D. Weet	E. Wet.
D. Wha	E. Who.
D. Whar	E. Where.
D. Whut	E. What.
D. Wid	E. Would.
D. Wid	E. Wood.
D. Windee	E. Window.
D. Winna	E. Will not.
D. Wirselz	E. Ourselves.
D. Wiyfee	E. Woman.
D. Wiz	E. Was.
D. Wiz	E. Us.
D. Wull	E. Will.
D. Wummin	E. Woman.

Y

D. Yaizd .... **E.** Used.

D. Yella .... **E.** Yellow.

D. Yi .... **E.** You.

D. Yit .... **E.** Yet.

D. Yull .... **E.** You will.

D. Yup .... **E.** Are you up? (Morning call.)

D. Yuv .... **E.** You have.

Z

D. Zat .... **E.** Is that.

D. Zit .... **E.** Is it.

D. Zitno .... **E.** Is it not.